The Human Side of Human Beings

of Human Beings

The Theory of Re-evaluation Counseling

By HARVEY JACKINS

The Human Side of Human Beings
The Human Situation
The Upward Trend
Fundamentals of Co-Counseling Manual
The Postulates of Re-evaluation Counseling
The Communication of Important Ideas
A New Kind of Communicator
The Complete Appreciation of Oneself
Who's in Charge?
The Flexible Human in the Rigid Society
The Logic of Being Completely Logical
Co-Counseling for Married Couples
The Nature of the Learning Process
The Uses of Beauty and Order
The Necessity of Long Range Goals
Multiplied Awareness
Letter to a Respected Psychiatrist
Is Death Necessary?
The Good and the Great in Art
The Distinctive Characteristics of Re-evaluation
      Counseling
Guidebook to Re-evaluation Counseling
"Quotes"
The Meaningful Holiday——poems
Zest is Best——poems
Rough Notes from Buck Creek I
Rough Notes from La Scherpa I
Rough Notes from Calvinwood I
Rough Notes from Liberation I & II

THE HUMAN SIDE
OF HUMAN BEINGS

The Theory of Re-evaluation Counseling

by Harvey Jackins

RATIONAL ISLAND PUBLISHERS

Seattle

First Printing	July, 1965
Second Printing	June, 1966
Third Printing	September, 1970
Fourth Printing	September, 1971
Fifth Printing	February, 1972
Sixth Printing	September, 1972
Seventh Printing	January, 1973
Eighth Printing	January, 1974
First Paperback Printing	September, 1972
Second Paperback Printing	January, 1973
Third Paperback Printing	January, 1974
Fourth Paperback Printing	November, 1974
Fifth Paperback Printing (revised)	May, 1975
Sixth Paperback Printing	December, 1975
Seventh Paperback Printing	August, 1976
Eighth Paperback Printing	April, 1977
Ninth Paperback Printing (revised)	March, 1978
Tenth Paperback Printing	December, 1978

ISBN No. 0-911214-60-7 (paper)
0-911214-62-3 (cloth)

Library of Congress Catalog Card No. 65-21901

The Re-emergent Human

At peace with all the universe
Yet filled with zestful fire,
Serene with past achievements,
Alive with new desire,
Aware of distant galaxies,
A pebble I admire.

The past informs and reassures.
The future beckons bright.
I face all human misery
And plan to set it right,
The genius of humanity
A constant, fresh delight.

I know the past and plan ahead
Yet live the now that's real.
I act by thought and logic.
I just feel the way I feel.
I don't confuse these separate things
Nor wind them on one reel.

What scars remain from long ago,
What fogs still clog my brain
Yield to the daily tears and yawns
That let me think again.
My use of all my gains includes
Continual further gain.

—Harvey Jackins

v

Contents

Acknowledgments

Gratitude is expressed here for assistance with this book and with the development of Re-evaluation Counseling theory.

First, appreciation goes to Mary McCabe, who has been my closest collaborator, has shouldered many difficult responsibilities and has made many original contributions to the theory.

Martha Remick, Margaret Loe and Margaret Hagerty, also, have shared responsibility for the thousands of hours of counseling people which established the workability and refined the concepts of the theory.

George and Harriet Gillies, Ruth Lochow, and Dorothy Lassers were of great assistance in the beginning. Many students and clients, far too many for the listing of their names, have inspired and continue to inspire us with their successes and with their persistent application of Re-evaluation Counseling theory in their varied lives and scattered locations.

Appreciation is due my family for their participation and support.

Irene McMahill has contributed greatly with typing and technical assistance.

Introduction

This book is an introduction to a theory of human behavior that marks a major breakthrough of human knowledge. It presents a solution to the basic problem of *human irrationality*, a problem which impedes the handling of all the other key questions now facing the world.

Human intelligence is defined concretely as the ability to construct a new, unique, accurate response to each new, unique experience which confronts each human at each moment of his/her existence.

This ability is differentiated explicitly from the ability of plants and animals to "choose" responses from an inherited, restricted list of pre-set response patterns.

Human irrationality is explicitly defined as failure to create and present such a new, unique, accurate response. It is presented as an acquired, non-inherent, unnecessary characteristic of present humans.

The source of human irrationality is located in the distress experiences which the human has undergone and has not been permitted to recover from completely.

The recovery processes, inherent and spontaneous in each human, are retrieved to view from the universal conditioned prejudice which has obscured them and are explicitly presented and described.

Ways of encouraging and assisting these recovery processes to completion and the results following from their use are indicated. These techniques and results are from the counseling practice of the author and his colleagues, a practice set up for the exploration and development of this theory.

This theory of human behavior is in sharp disagreement at many key points with other presently widely accepted theories, but not at any point where these other theories have produced practical results beyond "symptom suppression".

This book is an introduction only. Later publications will deal with the techniques of applying this theory with individual people and groups of people, and with its wide social implications.

Dec. 1, 1964

The Human Side
of Human Beings

The Theory of Re-evaluation Counseling

CHAPTER I

What to Expect

The following is a short description of what a human being may be like, in the important area of the human's response to the environment. It is a descriptive model of what *you* may be like, an attempt at a general guide to understanding all human beings and the source of their apparently contradictory activities.

This descriptive model has grown out of a deliberate and continuing attempt, now fourteen years in progress, to take a fresh look at human beings, to see what they are actually like without assumptions from past theories and models. This fresh look has been difficult to accomplish because of the depth and persistence of the suggestions with which all humans are burdened during our childhood and education years, but it has remained a clear goal during the period this model has been developed.

You may find this theory difficult to think about at important points where it is in sharp conflict with the theories you were expected to accept uncritically at your mother's knee, in Sunday school, from your psychology classes or from reading "psychological" fiction. The effort is worth making; these differences from older theories are among the most important things this description has to offer.

These differences require that this description be *thought about*. It cannot be accepted uncritically on the recommendation of any authority because it carries no such recommendation. The theory of Re-evaluation Counseling cannot be of much use to you *unless it makes sense to you!*

If this theory does make sense to you, it can happen that you find yourself uncomfortable about some of its implications, especially if you are a parent. Speaking as a parent, I can only say — "Welcome to the club."

In distinction to this description's differences with older theories, you may find it in remarkable agreement with your own experiences. It has been painstakingly assembled as the summary of actual experiences of hundreds of people.

2

I think you will find this descriptive model to be well-constructed. It assumes or defines a small number of simple concepts and these are related directly to common experiences on which there is general agreement. With these the model proceeds to a useful and consistent explanation of complicated and diverse phenomena.

This descriptive model leads directly to useful activity, to the tackling and solving of human problems, and provides consistent guidance for this activity. It leads continuously to the examination of new questions and to the opening of new fields of thought. New attitudes towards long-unsolved and vexing problems of human behavior, sociology and philosophy can appear as corollaries emerging from the central theses of this model.

You are likely to find this description of a human being useful to you, in the sense that you can cope with and solve certain problems that arise in living better with it than without it.

What follows is an outline of this theory.

CHAPTER II

Life versus Non-living Matter

This description begins with a comparison of the human's responses to the environment with those of other living things. *The responses of a human being to the environment resemble the responses of other living creatures more than they resemble the responses of non-living matter.*

This may seem obvious, but it is meaningful. Let us look at what we mean.

In general, non-living matter is passive in response to its environment. Give a chair a push and it is pushed. A billiard ball moves away from the cue-ball in a way largely determined by the momentum of the cue-ball, the angle of impact, the elasticity of the materials, etc. The general description of non-living matter's response to the environment is that it is passive, it is "pushed around" rather than "taking charge".*

The distinctive characteristic of living creatures, however, is exactly their *active* response to the environment. Living creatures tend to impose their organization on their surroundings. In the simplest, common-denominator way this is done by consuming a portion of the environment as food and reproducing. Thus a heap of relatively unorganized compost, when exposed to a pair of well-organized earthworms, will become converted in part and in time into a heap of organized earthworms.

Living creatures impose their organization on the environment in other ways besides ingestion and reproduction. The great Minnesota iron deposits, the chalk cliffs of Dover, the coral reefs of the Pacific are all sizeable structures achieved by the active, selective responses of certain microorganisms to the environment. The work of a

---

* (There are beginnings of active, organizing responses to the environment, even in non-living material. A seed crystal, for example, suspended in appropriate solution will "organize" the randomly oriented ions about it into a large crystal patterned after its own structure. Protoplanets will apparently grow into planets by attracting and accreting dust and debris from the primeval dust clouds. This is not the dominant behavior of non-living matter, however.)

colony of beavers can alter profoundly the surface geology of the valley they select for a dam.

Human beings, too, consume part of their environment for nourishment and, by reproduction, convert part of it into new human beings. Our numbers exceed three billion planet-wide. We are, *par excellence,* the living species that pushes the environment around in other complicated ways as well. We mine coal and metal, dam and bridge the rivers, terrace the hillsides, toss satellites into orbit, and prey upon all other species for food, raw material, decoration and sport.

To repeat, human beings are like other living creatures in their active responses to the environment more than they are like non-living matter with its overall passivity to the environment.

CHAPTER III

The Human Difference

Human beings are *different* from all other living creatures in the *kind* of active responses they make to the environment. What is this difference?

All living creatures with the exception of humans are able to respond actively to the environment only on the basis of *pre-set patterns of response*. These patterns are fixed in the heredity of the individual creature and are very similar to the patterns of other creatures of the same species or strain. The number of available patterns of response may be small for a simple creature and large for a complex creature, but the number of such patterns is finite and fixed in either case. These patterns can become disorganized and damaged during the lifetime of the individual creature, but they will not improve except through a process of maturation which is itself a pre-fixed response. A fine bird dog can have its delicate response patterns ruined by mistreatment, but the dog breeder will not expect better patterns of response than are called for by the particular dog's heredity.

These response patterns are usually called instincts, and the word is a good one if not carelessly applied to humans. When new response patterns do occur in a given hereditary line, this will be regarded as an evolutionary leap, a mutation. It will represent the emergence of a new strain or species.

Since the available patterns of response are fixed and limited in number for any one living creature other than a human, each such creature must categorize, i.e., it must meet a very large number of different environmental situations by lumping together those which are similar and meeting them with the same response. This type of behavior seems to have satisfactory survival value only for the species, not for the individual (speaking statistically).

One can apparently equate pre-set pattern (instinctive) behavior and species survival. When a given species' set of pre-set response patterns works well enough, that species survives. When it does not, that species dies out. Many species of

10

living things have died out in past times and their one-time existence is known to us only by their fossil remains.

This kind of behavior does not carry a very high survival value for the individual. It permits the species to survive only in association with massive reproduction rates.

A pair of codfish are reported to set about 14 million baby codfish adrift on the ocean currents each spawning season. Each of these baby codfish is equipped with the typical codfish assortment of pre-set response patterns. Each is able to respond to the environment only in codfish ways, not in ivy vine ways or butterfly ways.

These codfish response patterns certainly have worked well enough until now that there are still many codfish in the ocean. Yet the individual survival chances of one of these baby codfish would be far from what we would desire for ourselves, since, on the average, only *two* of these 14 million baby codfish survive to be parents of the next generation.

The overall behavior of all forms of life except human can be characterized as active response to the environment, a tendency to impress the surroundings with one's activity, but only on the basis of rigid, pre-set, inherent response patterns which can only roughly approximate the kind of behavior needed for survival in a particular circumstance.

A human being is different. The central feature of our humanness is a *qualitatively* different way of responding actively to the environment. Whether this essential difference was acquired by evolution or by creation makes no difference in understanding and using it.

This "human" ability seems to consist precisely of an ability to create and use *brand new*, unique responses to each new, unique situation we meet. When we are functioning in our distinctive human way we do not have to, nor do we, use any pre-fixed, inherent or previously worked out responses, but always and continuously create and use new precise responses that exactly match and successfully handle the new situation which we confront.

Let us stress this definition. We are not saying that a human being is *quantitatively* more complex in his/her behavior than an angleworm or a dog, in that the human can choose among a larger number of pre-set response patterns than lower animals can. We *are* saying that human behavior is *qualitatively* different than the behavior of other forms of life in that the human being can and does continuously *create new* responses all through the lifetime of the individual.

This essential difference has not been clearly faced in past theories or models. The long, persistent attempts by experimenters to understand human intelligence on the basis of their experiments with laboratory animals, for example, have led to more than one "dead end" school of psychology which explain everything about human beings except our "humanness" and which have been intuitively rejected by thoughtful people because of this.

We usually call this special human ability of ours our *intelligence*. This word is suitable and will generally be understood if we first draw a sharp line, as we have done above, between this flexible, creative, *human* intelligence and the rigid, pre-set responses of plants and animals. Intelligence in our human sense creates an endless supply of new, tailored-to-fit responses to the endless series of new situations we meet.

The behavior called "intelligence" in animals is based on categorizing, classifying and lumping together of different situations which are somewhat similar and meeting them with one rigid, pre-set response.

A moment's thought will make it clear that a human being never confronts an "old" situation. There are no identities in the physical universe, not even two electrons are identical. Certainly anything as complex as an environmental situation for a human will never be repeated exactly.

CHAPTER IV

The Operational Procedures of Intelligence

This special human ability of ours seems to work as follows:

(1) It continuously receives from the environment a great volume of information, coded in neural impulses, from the excellent battery of sense channels which each human possesses. This vast computer-like ability of ours receives many kinds of visual information from our eyes, many kinds of audible information from our ears and skull bones; it receives taste information, smell information, temperature information, balance information, and kinesthetic information from our many other sense organs.

(2) This vast volume of information coming into our intelligence is continuously and

quickly compared with the information already on file in what we usually call our memory, information from past experiences which we have already understood. Similarities between the incoming information and the information on file are apparently noted, as well as the ways in which similar experiences in the past have been successfully met.

(3) At the same time, this incoming information is *contrasted* with the information already on file; i.e., the differences are noted as well as the similarities. The incoming information is *understood* in relation to other information, in its similarities and differences to other data, not ever as a concept by itself.

(4) The information of how similar experiences were handled successfully in the past is used as a basis for constructing a suitable response to the present situation. The differences between the present situation and the similar past situations are, however, allowed for, and the actual response becomes tailored-to-fit the present exactly, as far as the available information allows.

16

(5) The new information from the current situation, having now been evaluated in terms of both its similarities and differences to other information, now goes on file in the memory as useful material with which to evaluate later experiences. We are better able to meet later experiences because of what we learned from the previous one. (This effect, for instance, will be very noticeable in beginning a new job in a new field. What is learned in the first week makes the second week comparatively easy to handle.)

This evaluation process is conducted both on aware and unaware levels. Usually the great bulk of evaluation takes place without aware attention, which is reserved for the most interesting or critical information. The assumption made in many theories that awareness and unawareness mark the boundaries between rational and irrational processes turns out to be misleading and is expressly *not* included in this description.

CHAPTER V

How Much Intelligence?

This ability, this flexible intelligence, is apparently possessed by each of us in such a very large amount as to be difficult for us in our present conditions to envisage.* Apparently if any of us could preserve in operating condition a very large portion of the flexible intelligence that each of us possesses inherently, the one who did so would be accurately described as an "all 'round genius" by the current standards of our culture.

This is not, of course, the impression that most of us have been conditioned to accept. We have heard, from our earliest age, that "Some have it and some don't", "Where were you when the brains were passed out?", "Don't feel bad, the world needs good dishwashers, too," and similar gems. These

* This capacity is destroyed or diminished permanently apparently only by physical damage to the forebrain.

impressions and this conditioning, however, seem to be profoundly wrong. Each of us who escaped physical damage to our forebrain began with far more capacity to function intelligently than the best operating adult in our culture is presently able to exhibit.

The adult who does function extraordinarily well compared to the rest of us, and whom we do call a "genius" in our admiration and respect, seems to be not someone who was endowed with extra ability to be intelligent when the rest of us were "hiding behind the door", but rather someone whom circumstances allowed to keep a considerable portion of his/her flexible intelligence functioning while everyone around him or around her was having theirs inhibited and interfered with.